Theo goes to Myanmar

Written by Oddny Gumaer
Illustrated by Elise Gumaer

Published 2018
Copyright © Oddny Gumaer 2018
© Partners Relief & Development
Chiang Mai, Thailand

www.partners.ngo

Printed in Chiang Mai, Thailand
by ActsCo
Text and layout by Oddny Gumaer
Cover and illustrations by Elise Gumaer

ISBN 978-616-455-471-9

This book is dedicated to all the children whose parents are working for Partners.
Thousands of children are thankful for the work your parents have done. We are thankful that you
have let us have your parents for this time in your life.

*Nathaniel, Tara, Nenana, Hunter, Hit, Heart, Fah Sai, Poom Jai, Joanna, Naam Pai, Naam Ping, Amm,
JaJa, Bai Bau, Thang Kwa, Naam Khing, Anna, View, Fluke, Ploy, Mi Mi, Arm, Guitar, Piano, Phop, Pai,
Olivia, Josiah, Erica, Amber, Brent, Maja, Emerson, Jude, Narelle, Avilyn, Carter, James, Hazel, Brian,
Lauren, Ross, Christopher, Catriona*

Your child is going on a journey

You may be joining, so here are some thoughts before the trip

Theo is going to take you on a journey through Myanmar, the nation in Southeast Asia that is so rich in history, beauty and diversity, and whose people are full of joy, hospitality and courage.

The story of Myanmar is full of sorrow, pain, losses and betrayal. For more than 50 years it was ruled by a military junta. Thousands of innocent people lost their lives during the oppressive rule, many more suffered terribly. And yet, the people did not, and still don't, give up hope. They are an example of resilience and bravery. Today, the nation still has its challenges. Human rights are challenged. Innocent children still die. However, we have chosen to focus on the things that set Myanmar apart in a good way—the culture, landscape and natural resources. There are a few mentions of the injustice and the atrocities, but not more than we found necessary. Although Aung San Suu Kyi has disappointed many people regarding her stand on human rights in the nation, we decided to include her in the book. She is currently the most famous and influential person from Myanmar. Our hope is that this book will help grow an awareness of the nation, and a desire for young people to love the people of this country.

Happy traveling

A
is for the Andaman Sea

This is Theo.
He is crossing the Andaman Sea. The Andaman Sea is the ocean surrounded by six different countries. The countries are Thailand, Malaysia, Myanmar, India, Sri Lanka and Indonesia. Theo is going to the country called Myanmar.

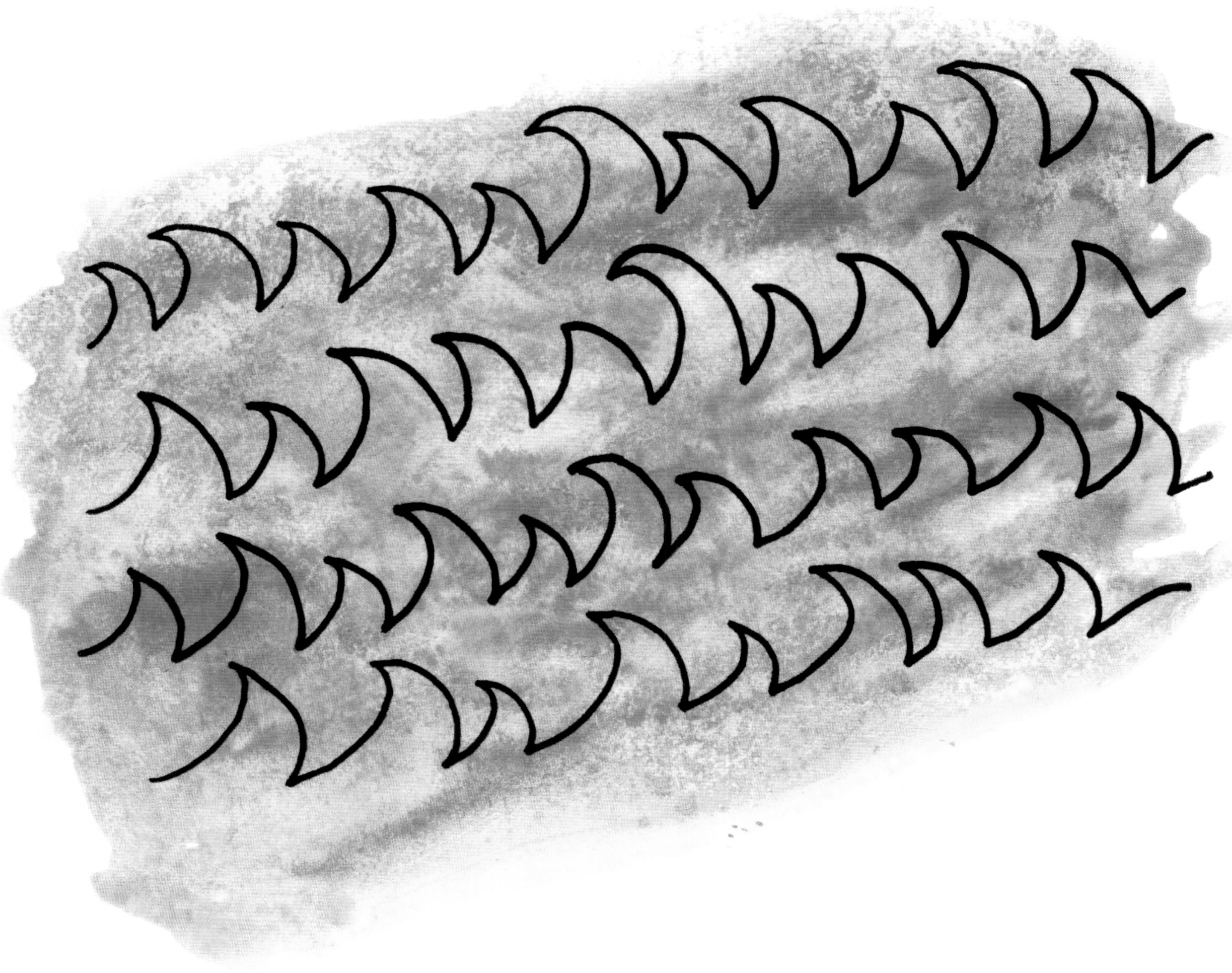

A
is also for Aung San Suu Kyi

When he gets to Myanmar he meets a man called Aung. He is going to be Theo's guide. First Aung shows Theo a picture of a lady called Aung San Suu Kyi. She is the most important lady in Myanmar. For many years she was under house arrest (that is kind of like being in prison). When she was released, many people voted for her and she became almost as important as the President.

B
is for banana

While in Myanmar, Theo eats lots of bananas. Some are short, some are long, and some are fat. Many of the bananas are different colors too. Who would have thought that bananas could be almost red? Theo learns that there are 25 different kinds of bananas in Myanmar. He also learns that people eat the banana flower. The flower is big and a little bitter. The banana leaves are also useful. They can be used for wrapping food instead of using plastic.

B
is for bamboo

Bamboo trees seem to grow everywhere. They make the country green. First, Theo learns that the bamboo is not a tree. It is a grass. The people in Myanmar use the bamboo for so many things. They build their houses with bamboo. They make furniture from bamboo. They also make mats, string, dishes, and paper. Some people even use bamboo to make clothes.

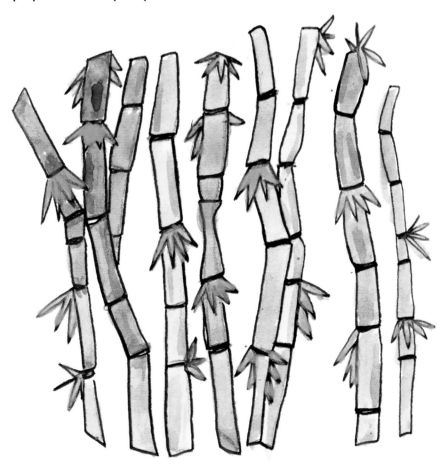

Belonging

All of us want to belong somewhere.
Which country do you belong to?
Write down some things you like about your country.
Perhaps you can think of one thing for each letter of the alphabet.

Do you belong anywhere else?
Think about where you belong and who you belong to. Imagine if you didn't belong anywhere? How would that feel?

Some children who have been forced to run from their homes are very sad because they don't feel like they belong anywhere. Some of them also feel like nobody wants them. They miss their homes and their school. They also miss the things that were familiar to them.

How can you help them or be their friend?

C
is for coconut

They walk past a coconut tree and Aung asks a boy to climb up in the tree to fetch a coconut. When the boy brings it down, Aung makes a hole in it and lets Theo drink the water that is inside! It tastes great. Coconut trees are some of the oldest trees in the world. They even existed in the time of the dinosaurs. The sweet coconut water is not just very tasty, it is also very healthy. Inside the coconut there is also the coconut meat which is delicious. The people in Myanmar make lots of different food with the coconut meat. They also dry some of it and grind it up to make flour. Then the coconut husk can be used to make fires and it is also used to make very strong rope. Finally, Aung tells Theo that the coconut palm leaves are the favorite food of elephants. "What a useful tree," thinks Theo.

D
is for dragon fruit

Theo is very surprised when he sees a dragon fruit. He isn't sure if it is a flower or a fruit. Then Aung tells him it is both. The dragon fruit is actually the flower of a cactus. The plant only blooms from evening to midnight, then it dies. During this short time, the flower is pollinated by moths or by bees, and a while later the beautiful dragon fruit is ripe. It tastes delicious and is very healthy.

Daring

Sometimes we must do the things we are afraid to do.
It could be to speak to a new child, or it may be to go to the dentist.
It could also be to eat a kind of food you have never tasted before.
It is good to learn to overcome our fears. That will make us stronger.

What are some things you are afraid of?
Would you like to overcome some of your fears?
How about trying to eat some new kinds of fruits? Are you brave enough?

In Myanmar, many children must do things they are afraid to do as well. Some children must hide from soldiers. Others must kill snakes. Some children must leave their villages and homes just to go to school. They miss their family, but since there are no schools in their village, they must move. Could you imagine that happening to you?

E
is for elephant

Aung lets Theo ride an elephant. Theo feels a little scared at first, but then he is OK. The elephant walks down to the river and fills her trunk with water that she sprays on herself and Theo. Theo laughs. Aung tells Theo that the trunk of the elephant has more than 100,000 muscles. They use their trunks for smelling, breathing, trumpeting, drinking, and also for grabbing things. The elephants of Myanmar even have fingerlike features at the end of their trunks so that it is easier to grab things. The elephants love to eat grass, roots, fruit and bark. In the past they were used for pulling logs and doing other work in the jungle. There are also many wild elephants in Myanmar. Unfortunately, many of them are disappearing because the humans cut down the jungle and the beautiful animals can't find enough to eat, and have nowhere to stay.

F
is for freedom

Aung takes Theo to talk to some people who fight for freedom in Myanmar. They tell Theo that the country used to be a dictatorship. That meant that the people who ruled didn't listen to what the people wanted and ruled the country in a bad way. Now Myanmar is not a dictatorship anymore, but many people are still suffering. Some are suffering because they are very poor. Others are suffering because the government doesn't like them. They don't have the same rights as the rest of the people because they have a different religion, because they look different, or because they have a different way of talking and dressing. Theo thinks this is very sad.

G
is for gecko

When Theo goes to bed he hears a strange sound above him. It sounds like something is calling out: "To-kay!" Aung takes him to see where the sound comes from. "It is a Tokay," he explains. The tokay is a kind of gecko that can be found everywhere in Myanmar. The one Theo gets to see is hiding on the beams in the ceiling of the house where they are staying. It is gtey, with red spots. Aung tells Theo that the gecko has millions of little pads and hairs under its feet. These make it possible for a gecko to walk on slippery glass, upside down from the ceiling, and even to hang upside down from one single toe. The geckos are awake at night and sleep during the day. They hunt for insects and like to eat cockroaches and locusts.

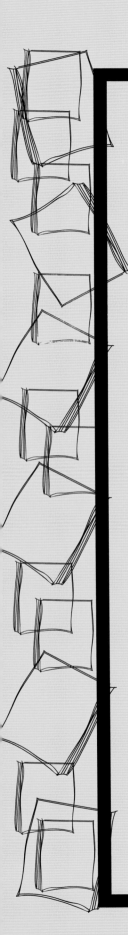

Goals

Goals help us focus.

Your goal could for example be to read this whole book without any help.
It could be to memorize some facts about Myanmar.
It could also be other things, such as learning the times tables or scoring a goal for your team.

Our big goal is that all children should have free and full lives. What do you think that means? Do you have a free and full life?

Try to set a new goal. Write it on a piece of paper and put it on your wall!

H
is for Hkakabo Razi

Today Aung and Theo fly to the north of Myanmar. They go to an ethnic state called Kachin. Here they will have a look at the tallest mountain in Myanmar, Mt. Hkakabo Razi. The mountain is 5,881 meters tall (19,295 feet) and is not just the tallest mountain in Myanmar, but the tallest in all of Southeast Asia. There is snow on the mountain, and it is very difficult to climb. The first person to get to the top of Hkakabo Razi was Takashai Ozaki from Japan in 1996.

I
is for Irrawaddy

After visiting Hkakabo Razi, Theo and Aung take a river trip on the longest river in Myanmar, the Irrawaddy. The Irrawaddy is 2,170 km long (1,350 miles) and runs from the north to the south of Myanmar. The Irrawaddy is very important for the people of Myanmar. Many people use it to bring goods from one place to another. They use boats to transport rice, wood, cotton and a lot of other things on the Irrawaddy. The most common boats on the river are called long-tail boats. People also use these boats to travel to many places. There are lots of animals and fish in the river. The most important animal in the Irrawaddy is the Irrawaddy dolphin.

J
is for jade

Aung and Theo go to a jade mine that also is in the north of Myanmar. Jade is a green stone that can be used to make jewelry, ornaments and tools. Many people, especially people from China, think that jade is the most beautiful rock because the green color is so pretty. They also think it will bring good luck, so they are willing to pay a lot of money for it. Aung tells Theo that Myanmar has some of the most beautiful jade in the world. Then he explains that because jade is so popular and expensive, people do crazy things to get it. In Myanmar, a few men and women think they can control the jade and get all the money for it. This makes the people living close to the jade mines poorer and poorer. Some people also die because they work in the dangerous mines. When digging for jade, the mountains and the nature in the area are destroyed as well.

Justice

We have justice when something is fair or right. We may say that something is not fair if we don't get our way.

But think about not being able to go to school, eat enough, or walk around freely just because you are poor, because you belong to a different people group or because you come from a poor country. When this happens, we need to work for justice.

Here are some things you can do to create justice:

Be kind. If we try to be kind to all the people we meet, we will make many people feel better.

Buy less stuff you don't need.

Be kind to nature. If we destroy our planet, it will make lives worse for the children living in poor places.

Give away your money. Find a charity you can give money to. They will spend the money to help children who live in poverty and whose lives are difficult for other reasons. You can also share your money with some people who need help in your own community.

K
is for Karen, Kachin, Karenni

Aung explains to Theo that Myanmar has many different people groups. By that he means people who speak different languages, wear different kinds of clothes, have different religions and different holidays and traditions. Three people groups start with the letter K:

The Karen

The Karen people are a part of one of the biggest people groups in Myanmar. There are about seven million Karen people altogether. The Karen live in a state called Karen State, or Kaw Thoo Lay in Karen language. They mostly grow rice, vegetables and raise animals for a living. They live in houses made from bamboo and thatch. Most Karen villages have a river or a stream nearby. That is where they take baths and do their laundry. For more than 50 years the Myanmar Army attacked the Karen villages and burned them to the ground. Therefore, many Karen people were forced to live in the jungle.

The Kachin

The Kachin people call themselves Jinghpaw. There are between 500,000 and one million Kachin people in Kachin State. The Kachin are mostly rice farmers who grow hill rice in the mountains. They are also famous warriors. The houses of the Kachin are often two stories, and oval shaped. The women dress in black jackets and colorful skirts. The men wear black, loose pants, a black jacket and a turban. Kachin state has a lot of natural resources, such as jade.

The Karenni

The Karenni people are often called The Red Karen. They come from the smallest ethnic state in Myanmar. The state has a lot of mountains. In the past, Karenni State also had a lot of teak and pine wood. But people have cut most of it down illegally. The Karenni are mostly farmers. They grow rice, millet, maize, sesame, garlic and vegetables.

L
is for Laphet Thoke

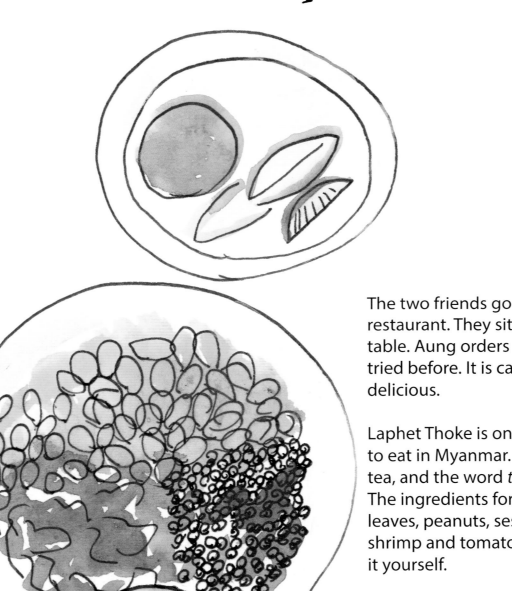

The two friends go to eat lunch at a local restaurant. They sit on low stools by a round table. Aung orders a dish that Theo has never tried before. It is called Laphet Thoke. It tastes delicious.

Laphet Thoke is one of the most common dishes to eat in Myanmar. The word *laphet* means green tea, and the word *thoke* means salad.
The ingredients for Laphet Thoke are: Pickled tea leaves, peanuts, sesame seeds, fried garlic, dried shrimp and tomato. Perhaps you can try to make it yourself.

M
is for moringa

"I will take you to the most powerful tree in the world," says Aung to Theo. Theo expects a big tree with a fat trunk. Instead, he sees a short tree that is skinny and has very small leaves. "This is the moringa tree," explains Aung. "Do you know that these leaves have much more protein than yogurt, lots more vitamin A than carrots, loads more potassium than bananas, a ton more calcium than milk, a bunch more vitamin C than oranges and heaps more iron than spinach?" Theo thought it was strange that such small leaves could hold so many good things. "And, guess what!" says Aung. "The seeds of the moringa can be used to purify water. It really is a miracle tree. Miracle moringa." In many villages where the people are poor, growing moringa will help them stay strong and healthy.

N
is for Naypidaw

To get to Naypidaw, the new capital of Myanmar, Theo and Aung must take a bus. When they arrive there, Theo is surprised. The city seems very modern and expensive. There are many fancy buildings and beautiful parks. Theo has never seen such wide roads. The strange thing is that there are hardly any cars on the wide roads. There aren't even that many people to see in Naypidaw. The Myanmar government and the Parliament meet at the government buildings in Naypidaw. Theo thinks it looks like nobody else really likes to be in the city.

O
is for ocean

"Today," says Aung, "we are going to the ocean." "There is an ocean in Myanmar?" asks Theo. He loves to swim. Aung tells Theo that the coastline in Myanmar is very long. 1,930 km to be exact. The oceans of Myanmar are full of all kinds of fish and mammals. If you are lucky you may spot the world's biggest fish, the whale shark, near one of the many islands. Aung and Theo see sea slugs, sea horses and sharks when they go diving off the coast. Not only that, but they get to see some of the most beautiful colored reefs. Theo thinks it looks like an underwater garden.

P
is for pagoda

When Theo and Aung travel across Myanmar, Theo notices beautiful golden structures. Tall towers rise high above the trees. They sparkle and shine, and often Theo hears the sound of tiny bells in the air. "We call them pagodas," Aung explains. "They are our Buddhist temples. In your country you have cathedrals. In Myanmar we have pagodas. The most famous of all the pagodas is the Shwedagon in Yangon. Many of our people call themselves Buddhists. We celebrate many Buddhist holidays. In our homes we also have small altars or shrines where we can give offerings to Buddha. And have you seen the Buddhist monks? They are always dressed in orange robes and their heads are shaven. We, the people of Myanmar, respect the monks and think of them as leaders of our society." Theo listens while he admires the pagoda next to them. "The people who built this must be very good and very patient," he thinks.

Q
is for queen

One day Aung takes Theo to the Mandalay Palace. Many tourists are there, taking pictures of themselves in front of the buildings. "Does the king live here?" asks Theo. Aung explains that nowadays they don't have a king, nor a queen, in Myanmar. But they used to. "The last king and queen in our country used to live here," he says. Theo wants to know their names. He learns that the king was named Thibaw, and the queen Supayalat. Aung tells Theo about the British making the country their colony, and the king and the queen being forced to flee to another country. They lived in India until the king died. Then Supayalat went back to live in Myanmar. She was very upset that she didn't get to be the queen anymore.

R
is for rice

"Let's go and eat some rice," Aung says to Theo when it is almost time for dinner. Theo is both surprised and disappointed that they are only going to eat rice since he is very hungry. "Is it normal that you just eat rice for dinner?" he asks. Aung starts to laugh. "I am sorry," he says. "When I say let's eat some rice, I mean: Let's eat something. In Myanmar rice is the most important thing we eat, and every meal has rice with it. For us, a meal without rice is not a meal. We say: Htamin Sar." After that, Aung tells Theo so many important things about rice. He tells him, for example, that rice is the most important food in the whole world. Two thirds of all the people in the world eat rice to live. Theo learns that rice needs a lot of water to grow. In fact, it will only grow when fields are full of water. Aung also says that only six countries in the world produce more rice than Myanmar. When Aung is done talking, Theo is so hungry, he eats two plates full of rice. And some vegetables too, of course.

R
is for Rohingya

In Western Myanmar Theo meets some people who look very different than the other people he has met in the country. "They are the Rohingya," explains Aung. "The Rohingya are a people group who have lived in Myanmar for many hundreds of years. They are Muslims, and their skin color is dark." Theo thinks they are beautiful. "The sad thing about the Rohingya is that many of the people in my country don't want them here. For many years, they have been trying to get rid of them, saying that they don't belong here. Many have been killed, their homes were destroyed and now most of them have escaped from the country." Theo is shocked. How can this be? He looks at a little Rohingya child and wonders why some people think she doesn't belong in the country she was born in.

S
is for Shan

Theo and Aung have ended up in the Shan hills. The temperature is cooler than in the central areas of the country. "The Shan are one of the many people groups in Myanmar. They have lived in what is called Shan State for many thousands of years. Shan State is very big—around one fourth of all the land in Myanmar. Nobody knows exactly how many Shan people there are, but we think there are between four and six million Shan in Myanmar." Aung tells Theo that most of the Shan people are rice farmers, but that many also grow tea. "When you go to visit some Shan in their house, they will always serve you a cup of tea," explains Aung. He also tells Theo that most of the Shan follow the Buddhist religion, and that they celebrate many Buddhist holidays. They also have their own language, Shan. Unfortunately, many Shan are not able to attend school so they don't learn to read and write. Another problem is that there are not enough doctors, nurses and medicine in Shan state.

T
is for thanaka

Theo is a little surprised to see that so many of the people he saw in Myanmar have painted their faces in a pale yellow color. At first he thinks they are going to a party, but he understands that people will paint their faces this way every day. He asks Aung what the paint is, and why so many people wear it. "We call the paint thanaka," explains Aung. "It is actually a tree." "A tree!?" Theo is very surprised to hear this. "Yes, we grind the bark from the thanaka tree and mix it with a little bit of water. We spread it on our faces because we think it looks beautiful. But not only that, it also cools our skin when it is very hot outside. It works a little bit like the sunscreen you use in your country. Also, we believe that thanaka gives us smooth skin. You should try it yourself," he smiles, and puts some thanaka on his fingers and paints a pretty design on Theo's face.

Transform

To transform means to change. A caterpillar transforms into a butterfly. Trees in the spring transform too. They have no leaves in the winter, but then, when spring comes, the leaves come out and transform the tree. We also transform. We grow and become bigger. We lose our teeth and get new ones. We learn to read and ride our bicycles. Sometimes we are not very kind. If we practice being kind, we will transform into a kinder person.

What are some transformations that have happened in your life? Look at pictures of yourself from some years ago and try to write down all the changes.

Do you think that you could transform the life of someone else?
we think you could.

Imagine transforming the whole world. What are some things that have transformed the planet we live on?

U
is for umbrella

Theo sees women carrying umbrellas over their heads even though it is not raining. "It is just as normal to carry an umbrella to protect from the sun as it is to protect from the rain," says Aung. "Women don't like their skin to turn dark. Also, it is always so hot, and the umbrella gives us a little bit of shade. It is one of the most useful possessions people own. Just imagine! Half of the year we need it because of the monsoon season. The other half of the year we need it because of the hot sun. Nowadays we can buy umbrellas that were made in factories, but in older days we had them handmade and hand painted. Some of the umbrellas were beautiful pieces of art. You can still get those kinds of umbrellas, but they are very expensive and not very useful."

V
is for visiting

One day Theo and Aung get invited to the house of some of Aung's relatives. Before they walk inside, they remove their shoes. They put them at the bottom of the stairs outside the house. Once inside, they sit down on the floor. Aung explains to Theo that the carpet on the floor is not for walking on. It is more like the dining table and shortly everybody sits around the carpet eating delicious food. Theo learns that in Myanmar one must be careful not to point one's feet at anybody. People will think that is very impolite since the feet are the lowest part of the body. But when he becomes good friends with one of the girls in the house, he learns it is fine to play with her the same way he plays with his friends back home.

W
is for wildlife

Theo loves animals and asks Aung to take him on another trip to Hukaung Valley in Kachin State. The area is the largest tiger reserve in the world. The government in Myanmar was worried that because so many people hunted the tigers in the country, they would soon all die. Now the tigers can live in peace in Hukaung Valley. Theo thinks it is nice and exciting. He walks into the forest with Aung. They are very quiet and try to spot a tiger. They don't see any, but instead they see a deer, and in the trees they hear monkeys chatting. Theo thinks he sees a couple of them. And they see lots of beautiful birds. Aung says that Myanmar has so many kinds of animals. There are tigers and leopards, elephants and rhinoceros, wild buffalos and boars, monkeys, crocodiles, turtles, and many kinds of snakes. There are at least 100 different kinds of birds, too. Many of them are very colorful. "The sad thing is that too many people are hunting our animals to get food and money," says Aung. "They don't understand that if they keep doing that, we will soon have no wild animals or birds left in our beautiful forests." Right before they leave the green jungle of Hukaung Valley they hear branches breaking. They squat down behind a bush. There, not far from them they see a large tiger walking past. "Be safe," whispers Theo.

X
is for Xerox

For many years the government of Myanmar made it illegal to buy and read many books that the government didn't like. The government wanted to decide what the people should read. During that time the people of Myanmar would smuggle illegal books into the country and Xerox many copies of the books on copy machines. They would sell the books to anybody who wanted them in secret. If the police or government officials noticed it, the people selling the books might get arrested. Theo hears this from Aung and he thinks it is crazy that people would not be allowed to read whatever they wanted, and that you could be put in prison for selling the wrong kind of books. He wonders if his favorite book *Where the Wild Things Are* had been forbidden.

XOXO

Perhaps somebody has written you a note and ended it with "xoxo." That is a way to write hugs and kisses.

It is nice when somebody loves us so much they give us hugs and kisses. Our parents mostly love us that much. Who are some other people who love you very much? Write their names on a list and be thankful for all the good people in your life.

It is important to remember that even though people are poor and don't have a lot of things, they love their children just as much as your parents love you. They don't like it when their children don't have enough to eat, or can't go to school.

we must make it so that families can stay together and that their children can live with their parents even though they are poor. Sometimes the parents are so poor they send their children away to live at an orphanage. Imagine how sad that is.

Y
Yangon

Theo's trip is coming to an end. Before he goes back, Aung wants to take him to the old capital of Myanmar, Yangon. Although it is no longer the capital of the country, it is still the largest and most important city. Aung says they have to spend the day well because there is lots to see. They start the day by eating breakfast at one of the road-side tea shops. They sit on short stools on the sidewalk while they dip their fresh breadsticks, *e kya kway*, into the sweet tea.

After breakfast they go to the most famous market in Yangon, the Bogyke Aung San market. Here Theo buys some gifts for his family. He buys a lacquerware bowl for his mom, a Burmese puppet on strings for his sister, and a cotton longyi for his dad, the same kind Aung and most Burmese men wear. The market buzzes with activity and there is no way they have time to stop by all of the 2,000 shops. Instead, they go to the center of the city and take a look at a building that is right in the middle of a large intersection where cars and rickshaws rush by. "This is the Sule Paya," says Aung about the octagonal-shaped building. "It was built 2,000 years ago. Do you know why? To have a place to store one of Buddha's hairs."

They walk around the city a bit and notice how all the street signs are written with the Burmese alphabet, and how people walk to and fro wearing thanaka on their faces, and smiling with smiles reddened by the betel nut most of them chew. They take a taxi to a big lake on the outskirts of the city, Inya Lake. Lots of other people have gathered here for their lunch breaks. Theo notices that many are boyfriends and girlfriends and they sit on the ground holding each other's hands. Theo and Aung lay down in the shade and rest. Late in the afternoon, as the sun is about to set, they arrive at the Shwedagon Paya. The most famous pagoda in the country, perhaps in the whole world. The pagoda sparkles in the sun, and as the sun is setting it looks almost like it is on fire. Aung tells Theo that more than 27 tons of gold covers the pagoda. And not only that, there are also thousands of diamonds and other gems on the pagoda. Theo thinks it is beautiful and walks on bare feet while he admires the beautiful building. He sees so many people who take the time to kneel and pray.

Z
ZZZZ

Theo has had such a busy and interesting time in Myanmar. His head is full of thoughts and stories to tell when he goes home. He hugs Aung goodbye. Aung hugs him back, but then shows him how to say goodbye in the proper way in Myanmar. He puts his palms together as in prayer, lifts them up to his face and nods slightly. "Goodbye, Theo," he says and walks away. Theo is so tired that he falls asleep as soon as he is sitting on the plane. He doesn't even see the Shwedagon Pagoda lit up with thousands of lights as the airplane flies over the city. "Zzzzzz," says Theo.

Finally

We hope you enjoyed the journey through Myanmar and that you learned a lot.

If you would like to help the children of Myanmar get free, full lives, you should check out Partners Relief & Development (we just call ourselves Partners for short). Partners has worked in Myanmar for many years. We have helped many hundreds of thousands of people. In the areas of the country where children (and adults) don't have food, medicines or shelter, Partners provides. In the villages and towns where people need help to grow their own food, or help to get jobs, Partners helps. We call it sustainable development. And in places where children don't have the opportunity to go to school, or sick people don't have hospitals to go to, Partners starts schools and clinics. We call it strengthening communities.

Perhaps you want to help Partners do the important work they are doing.
Find out how on our website: www.partners.ngo

You can of course follow us on social media as well. Check us out on Instagram, Twitter and Facebook.

Oddny Gumaer founded Partners Relief & Development with her husband Steve. She is a popular speaker and the author of three books. She is the mother of Elise Gumaer.
Elise Gumaer was born in Thailand and spent much of her childhood with refugees from Myanmar. She currently lives and studies in Norway.